[explicit lyrics]

Miller Williams Poetry Series
EDITED BY BILLY COLLINS

[explicit lyrics]

Poems by Andrew Gent

The University of Arkansas Press

FAYETTEVILLE ■ 2016

ISBN: 978-1-55728-695-6

e-ISBN: 978-1-61075-581-8

20 19 18 17 16   5 4 3 2 1

Text design by Ellen Beeler

♾The paper used in this publication meets the minimum requirements of the American National Standard for Permanence of Paper for Printed Library Materials Z39.48-1984.

Library of Congress Control Number: 2015952480

For Lauretta

Series Editor's Preface

When the University of Arkansas Press asked if I would act as editor for the coming year's annual poetry prize named in honor of Miller Williams, the press's cofounder, long-time director, and progenitor of its poetry program, I was quick to accept. Since 1988 when he published my first full-length book, *The Apple That Astonished Paris*, I have felt indebted to Miller, who died in January 2015 at the age of eighty-four.

When he first spotted my poetry, I was forty-six years old with two chapbooks only. Not a pretty sight. I have him to thank for first carrying me across that critical line dividing *no book* from *book*, thus turning me, at last, into a "published poet." I was especially eager to take on this task because it is a publication prize that may bring to light other first books. In fact, from the beginning of his time at the press, it was Miller's practice to publish one poet's first book every year. Then in 1990 this commitment was formalized when Miller awarded the first Arkansas Poetry Prize. Fittingly, it was renamed the Miller Williams Poetry Prize after his retirement and has grown to welcome work from both published and unpublished writers alike.

Miller Williams was more than my first editor. Over the years, he and I became friends, but even more importantly, before my involvement with the press, he served as a kind of literary father to me as his own straightforward, sometimes folksy, sometimes witty, and always trenchant poems became to me models of how poems could sound and how they could go. He was one of the poets who showed me that humor could be a legitimate mode in poetry—that a poem could be humorous without being silly or merely comical. He also showed me that a plain-spoken poem did not have to be imaginatively plain. Younger poets today could learn much from his example, as I did.

Given his extensive and distinguished career, it's surprising that Miller hasn't enjoyed a more prominent position on the American literary map. As his daughter became well known as a singer and recording artist, Miller became known to many as the father of Lucinda Williams. Miller and Lucinda even appeared on stage together several times performing a father-daughter act of song and poetry. And Miller enjoyed a bright, shining moment when Bill Clinton chose him to be the inaugural poet at his second inauguration in 1997. The poem he wrote for that day, "Of History and Hope," is a meditation on how "we have memorized America." In turning to the children of our country he broadens a nursery rhyme question by asking "How does our garden grow?" Occasional poems, especially for occasions of such importance, are notoriously difficult—some would say impossible—to write with success. But Miller rose to this lofty occasion and produced a winner. His confident reading of the poem before the nation added cultural and emotional weight to the morning's ceremony.

Apart from such public recognitions, most would agree that Miller's fuller legacy lies in his teaching and publishing career, which covered four decades. In that time, he published over a dozen books of his own poetry and literary theory. His accomplishments as a writing poet and working editor are what will speak for Miller in the years to come. The qualities of his poems make them immediately likeable and pleasurable. They sound as if they were spoken, not just written, and they show a courteous, engaging awareness of the presence of a reader. Miller knew that the idea behind a good poem is to make the reader feel something, rather than to merely display the poet's emotional state, which usually boils down to some form of misery. Miller also possessed the authority of experience to produce poems that were just plain wise.

With these attributes in mind, I began the judging of this year's prize. On the lookout for poems that Miller would approve of, that is, poems that seemed to be consciously or unconsciously in the Miller Williams School, I read and read. But in reading these scores of manuscripts, I realized that applying such narrow criteria would be selling Miller short. His tastes in poetry were clearly broader than the stylistic territory of his own verse; he published poets as different from one another as John Ciardi and Jimmy Carter. I readjusted and began to look for poems I thought Miller would delight in reading, instead of echoes of his own poems. This took some second-guessing, but I'm confident that Miller would enthusiastically approve of this year's selections.

Broadening the field of judgment brought happy results. The work of four very different poets, who have readability, freshness of language, and seriousness of intent in common, stood out among the stack of submissions.

Andrew Gent's *[explicit lyrics]* is a fascinating collection of poems that slip through their own cracks and seem to vanish before the reader's eyes. Influences are a matter of guesswork, but I'd say he has learned some of his admirable tricks from Yannis Ritsos and some of the New York School. Surprises lurk on almost every page. *See You Soon,* the casual title of Laura McKee's book, contains poems of powerful feeling that seem composed in the kind of tranquility of recollection, which Wordsworth recommended. Living in a country that appears to be continually involved in war on many fronts, readers will find in Brock Jones's *Cenotaph* a new way of thinking and feeling about the realities of combat. It is difficult to write war poetry because the subject is pre-loaded with emotional weight, but Jones more than manages to render precisely the mess of war with tenderness and insight. Joe Wilkins's poems are located in the tradition of the sacred, but holiness here is found in common experience. *When We Were Birds,* as the title indicates, is full of imaginative novelty as well as reminders that miraculous secrets are hidden in the fabric of everyday life.

In short we have here a gathering of young poets whose work, I think, would have fully engaged and gladdened Miller Williams. Because I have sat with him there, I can picture Miller in his study turning the pages, maybe stopping to make a pencil note in a margin. Miller's wider hope, of course, was that the poems published in this series would find a broad readership, ready to be delighted and inspired. I join my old friend and editor in that wish.

—Billy Collins

Contents

[explicit lyrics]

Dead Mouse

The only good mouse.
But not pretty
to look at.

Its neck and lower half
of its head crushed.
The legs splayed out
like a fat man
taking a belly flop
into the neighbor's pool.

But little if any blood
and all the pieces
still attached.
You are afraid
to touch it.

What you know to be
dead, your primal brain fears
may be faking it, could
suddenly spring to life
as you reach for it.

Then what? Mouse vs. man
mano-a-mano action?
Logic precludes
what the mind fears
but the mind wins out.

Until gloves and a quick flip
into a plastic bag
finish the job.

Not very manly,
but danger (even imaginary)
averted. The fur,
the black eyes,
the look of surprise.
All these

are things
you must work
to forget.

Hiroshige

What once were trees
are now a few quick brush strokes.

What once was a bridge
is now the absence of paint

as if snow were erasing
what we have built.

What once were mountains
are now vanishing in the mist

as if the world we knew
were a delicate thing.

Nail

Rust's patron saint.
Butt of a million bad jokes.

The drum that cannot be played.
A machine that never stops.

Fossil,
and the tool

that will uncover it.

Lightbulb

A Henry Moore sculpture
of a snake, coiled.

The long tail of light
approaching from a distant star.

Everything, anything
exhausted, colorless.

There could be a river inside.
Trees, sky. All painted in white.

Lightbulb

X-ray of an alien being.
The round, bald,
featureless head
lit from inside.

A millennium of scientific research
shrinking the cortex
down to a single coil.
But ultimately, fragile.

Which is why it is here
covered by a white cloth,
casting ominous shadows
on the living room wall.

Kayak for Sale

My neighbor is selling his kayak.
The one he loaded onto his car
at 8:00 a.m. every Saturday morning.
Then he would return late in the afternoon,
rinse it off with a garden hose and put it away,
for a week. But he is retired now.
His children have grown up
and away, and recently
he sold his wife's car. Obviously
thinking they need just one car now
that only she works. But I never
expected that he would be
propping his orange kayak
up on two lawn chairs in the side yard
with a hand-drawn sign saying "For Sale".
Is it finally too much work? Too tiring?
Or did he never really like it?
That chore done, he gets out the bucket and hoses
and starts to wash the car for the second time
this week. Every once in a while
he pauses to examine the sponge
in his hand, wondering
if that too should soon go.

I Have Suffered

I have suffered the trees
their light, their radiant
fruit. I have suffered
their errant branches
and coarse skin. I have
had words with their gnarled
roots in the dark of night.
I have begged, I have wept.
I have thrown myself
at their mercy. For what,
you might ask? For naught.
For the nothing
they demand or allow
for their being here
or that they expect
of our being as well.
We, the beasts of prey
they shelter and surfeit.

Babel

Where lang-
uage goes
we follow
like sheep
each drawn to
its own mother
tongue. Bleat.

Bleat. The clouds
look like sheep
drawn by hand.
We follow each
other up

the tower
where the clouds are
said to live. But
our own tongues
cannot tell us

what they are
called. Swollen
with words
they (tongues)
betray us

like sheep
left to stray
where we
should know

danger is.

Laundry

So much of what I own
ends up here, waiting
to be reclaimed.

Crumpled, soiled
abandoned.

Just as if
Michelangelo's David
were to return to a lump of stone.

And you expect the old Vietnamese lady
behind the counter
to bring it back to life.

"Day after tomorrow" she says
and hands you a ticket.

As if time is all that is needed

and the strange machinery you hear
behind the curtain.

Crow

He has the profile
of a Roman emperor
or an Egyptian god.
What we imagine
lurks inside the skull
when we are alone at night.
The pages of a book
burnt beyond recognition.
The words of the author
collected like a pile of ashes
where a minute before
it rested on the bookshelf.
Sorrow's plaything.
Misery's youngest daughter.

Mosquito

Evolution driving
down a blind alley.
All legs and needle
on one side. On the other,
wings and compound eye.
The laboratory
of its own making.
The final experiment
before a terrible discovery.

Out of Sleep

I was dreaming
the doorbell
rang.
Was it real
or a dream?
Forced myself
awake,
downstairs
to open the door, but
no one was there.
Only
the sound of birds
and my neighbor
turning
from his pre-dawn
preparations
for a fishing trip
to smile and wave.
Who was it?
Real or imagined,
who was so desperate
to reach me?
And what
was the hurry
they couldn't wait
for me
to unlock the door?

I wave back
like the ghost
I will be
someday.

How to Clean an Oil-Slicked Penguin

Like the punch line to a very bad joke
the obvious and actual answer
is: "carefully".
First, you must learn to hold the penguin
from behind, to avoid the beak,
pressing both wings against the body
until you need to hold each out
(again, carefully) to clean
in and around the extremities.
Next, contrary to logic,
you apply more oil
(cooking oil works best)
to loosen and remove
the thicker crude. Working it (carefully)
into the feathers. Next
you clean what remains
with dishwashing detergent
four, five, maybe even six times.
Careful (yet again) to avoid
the eyes and mouth.
You want to clean the feathers
without removing their natural
protective coating, or else
the penguin will sink like a stone
having lost its normal buoyancy.
Finally, you let it rinse off
in a pool of clean water.

Let the penguin do the work,
preening its coat and reclaiming
what little remains of its dignity.
Do not expect thanks.
In fact, it will continue
to bite and scratch.
But, if you are lucky,
it might survive.
Which is the most
we can hope for.

Repairs

Don't tell me the branch is dead.
Tell me the tree is healthy.
Tell me lies I can use.
Explain that four months of ice and storm
are healing. That amputation
is a way to keep the body clean
rather than the inevitable
result of age.
Tell me
you will make better
what is not well. Write it
somewhere
in your elaborate scrawl
on the pink estimate sheet
you hand me.

On Beauty

I am attracted
to the purely physical:
the female anatomy,
the salient parts
mostly, but not quite
disguised by a shred
of black cloth
and laid out
in a chair next to the pool.

Why not?
What is designed
to attract, attracts.
(Bees to honey, etc. . . .)
But I am not a bee
and she is not honey.
And as much as I
might hate to admit it
she is not (and should not
be) interested in me.
The attraction is purely art.

Well, art and desire.
Which I cannot—
for the life of me—
distinguish between.

No Sign of Relief in Sight

Someone fell off their back porch
and their porch fell with them.
Termites, someone said.
Lousy construction, another
speculated. Too many
people, you know
they must have been
having a party. Their own
damn fault. I suspect
any of them might be true
but the person falling
was not thinking
cause & effect
as he fell. He was thinking
"I am not that drunk.
I did not fall down
but I am falling
and the ground
is going to hurt
me."

Healing

"How can I bring my aching heart to rest?"
                                        —Li Fu-Jen

Go abroad. Buy a pet. Find a field
overgrown with brambles, clear it by hand,
plant it with nasturtium and hollyhock
and wait for them to grow.

Learn to whittle
replicas of the twelve animals
that make up the Chinese calendar.

Sit perfectly still
in a dark room
concentrating
until you can feel the earth
moving under you.

If (and when) that fails
learn to accept
what you cannot believe
right now: that
only the heart
can heal itself.

Overheard

"I used to care
because I thought it made a difference.
Pffft! Love me,
or not. It doesn't matter.
You act like the same
fucking jerk either way . . ."

January Thaw

Little sorrows peck at the ground.
Hippity hop, my grieving ones!
A distant star expires
radiating a cold light.
The world thinks in clichés:
January is covered in a fine dust.
It is already too late
to start over . . .
Think of the future:
ten years from now
what was dead
will come back to haunt you.
Look! The brown-headed one
has found a candy wrapper
to fret over. The fine print
erased from being outside so long.
His fellow mourners are jealous
but they cannot stop
their dance of joy.

Glass of Milk

X-ray of the heart,
overexposed.

A map of Antarctica.
Antarctica itself.

Sorrow's little sobriquet.
Darkness, having turned the corner.

Rock

1.

Dinosaur egg.
Early attempt
at the wheel.
Accompanied by string
and a hand-written note,
message and messenger.
A piece of a star
extinguished millions of years ago.

2.

Telephone for the deaf.
Both a rock and a hard place.

Ancient runes.
Premonition.

Dice for a game
no one can remember.

Evolution of Rock

Not exactly the world's most interesting
biography: rock. rock. rock.
Then, during the last ice age
it moves house to the side of a hill
in what will become New Hampshire.
At some point a crack appears:
youthful games, a traumatic accident, or just old age.
Whatever the story, the stone's not telling.
Moss gathers
on the north side
and someone has put up a sign: Glacial Erratic.
Strange name for a rock.
But then, it is
busy thinking
out its next move.

Shopping Cart

Chicken coop on wheels.
A prestidigitator's living room.
Smoke from the ants' many factories.
Skeleton of a Roman chariot.
What my father has been working on
in the basement all these years.
My mother's escape pod
from this planet to the next.
Crate.
Sign.
Omen.

Seven Juncos in the Backyard

How do they do it?
Perched like acrobats
swaying and unswayed
by the least hint
of wind.

Street performers, party hats

thrown into the trees
each with a child's name written
by hand. We wish
we had that kind of joy,
that abandonment

to the laws of physics.

We can recite the reasons
not to. But somehow
it feels foolish
to argue the plausible
in the face of the improbable.

So what?

What was important at eighteen
or even twenty-something
is ancient history twenty-five years later.

They are the clowns
we refused to become

hopping through the backyard,

stopping to peck at a seed
or scrap of grass, oblivious
to the bucket of confetti
about to be hurled
in their direction

as we, the bystanders

sit riveted to our seats
in the bleachers, our faces painted in
portraits of shock and surprise.

Candidate

His smile is borrowed from his ancestors:
the executioner, the circus barker,
the late-night hotel desk clerk.
He recites books he has read—or written—
one sentence at a time. Repeating them
over and over as if familiarity
begets truth rather than contempt.
Behind him you can hear the sound
of knives being sharpened,
bones being broken,
and large vats of detritus
being emptied into the street
behind an abattoir.

Spilled Milk

I won't go into the reasons to cry
over it. Where it came from . . .
How it has been mistreated . . .
For the moment, let's take it at face value.
The white map of a lake you imagine
surrounded by trees, a few cabins,
and to the south, a highway
almost touching the shore.
If you look closely
you can make out the half-submerged docks
waiting for canoes and swimmers
fresh from the water.
But it must be winter: the lake is white
and there is no one here.
At the edges you find other tracks
(crumbs perhaps) where deer
have come to lick the ice
and stare into the round face of the moon
or their own same-as-in-death
reflections.

Plant

One of the few things
that does not wither up and die
when I bring it home.
Hardy. Immune
to darkness and lack
of water. (A result of forgetfulness
not abuse.) But all the same
to the green, rooted being
I call my own. This one
is happy (I think)
to spread its flat
waxy leaves and be still.
Happy for what sustenance
I give it. And I, in return,
am happy to see
it each morning,
impossibly green
in the half light
of where I carry on.

Reading a Chinese Poet

There is no poetry in the words
by which I assume he meant "woods".
Because there is no poetry
in the woods, just music.
The leaves opening and closing
their clarinet cases. The sparrows
constantly adjusting their chairs.
Until the wind taps his baton
three times. Nothing but music.
Whereas words are full of meaning,
which when you play them
make a sound not unlike poetry.

Crow

The crow's name
is Ted. Unhappy

Crow. Unlucky
to be born

a writer. Ted lived
like a crow.

Crows do not have friends.
Crows think about

themselves first,
and everything else

later. Ted realized
a crow's life

was hard on his wives.
They had black thoughts.

The crow in him
couldn't see the forest

for the trees.
Be happy,

he said. Life
is supposed to be hard

for a crow.

Movies

You know, it's like a movie
you've seen—I dunno,
some x years ago—and remember
each and every scene
as if it were your own life
played out in Technicolor.
You tell all your friends
about it like it was
Citizen Kane, Casablanca,
and *400 Blows* all rolled into one.
Then—what do you know—
it shows up on television.
You make special arrangements
to stay up and watch it
(you even make popcorn)
and . . . What the hell!?
This isn't the movie
you remember. The "hero"
is chewing the scenery
and the girl is nothing
you could call
beautiful. Your life
wasn't anything like this.
How could you get it
so wrong? You shake
your head in the dim glow
of the screen, which could be

a scene from another famous movie
your life resembles, whether you like it
or not.

Don't Tell Me about Love

Talk to me about the weather
in El Paso, Texas
and how many transfers
it takes to get there by bus.
Tell me how you met Bob Marley,
how you sold him dope,
and where you got that scar
above your left ear.
Lie to me
about anything
but don't

tell me about love.

Political Poem

The knife despises the fork.
The fork is the proletariat in this story.
It does all the work, the heavy
lifting and carrying.
But the knife, the knife thinks,
does the important work.
It does things no one else can do.

The knife has a lot to say
but no one is listening.

Saying

Early bird gets the worm.
Night owl misses out.
Friends say jaybird misunderstood.
A sorry tale of jealousy.
The early bird told local news
his secret to success:
hard work, etc.
The worm, rumor has it
collects welfare, cheated
on his taxes, entered
the country illegally.
(On his belly, so to speak.)
I'm just saying . . .

Dreams

My dreams are small enough to fit in this matchbox.
Several of them are caught under my fingernail.
Others drift like dust motes through the sunlight
that always brightens this room. It is
early afternoon. It is Summer,
the year: 1973.
I am waiting for something
I cannot remember right now.
While I wait, I let them out
and play with them, holding each
by its tiny wings, laughing
at its struggles.

Wake

The boat comes ashore with it
like proof of a story we don't believe.
This large . . . that fast . . . Got away.
The slap of the waves
tells you something happened
and someone is not telling the truth.

Old Age

Like Beethoven going deaf
one note at a time,
I am going blind
line by line. At first
the fine print escaped
from instruction manuals
and prescription bottles.
Then newspapers and magazines.
Now even poetry is nothing more
than a collection of stones
round, hard, and indecipherable
arranged on the white sand
of the blank page.

Inner City

The machine that manufactures dreams
stands idle on the far side of the river.
The shadow of a shadow. No one
works there anymore. But
they have plans to replace it.
Make it bigger, better,
more efficient, and fully automated.
With no need for human
interference. The machine
can manufacture its own dreams.
Dreams of when people
still roamed the earth.

Weather

The grass tells its story with a thousand voices.
The woodpecker has only one.
They are boarding up the windows in sparrow town
using straw and bric-a-brac.
Bad weather's coming.
My wife says she can smell it
like the scent of fox or coyote—
all wet fur and the hair standing up
on the back of her arm. I spoke too soon.
It is a coyote: large, dark, and wet
crouching on the horizon
disguised as nothing more
than a line of clouds.

Depression

The tropics have sent us
bad juju. Wind & rain
with its name on it.
The windows streak and blur
like old-age glass
(what they call "bull's eye")
as we try to see through water
to the familiar
back yard
now ankle deep in the stuff.
But this insistence
on darkness has its good points:
The burning bush
too early in the season
to be red, practically glows
against the darker green
of pine and oak
that backdrops this scene.
We will survive the minor damage
this storm inflicts: tree limbs down,
flower pots swept away, a broken window.
But the colors we imagine
cannot endure.

Pornography

Clowns in flesh-colored suits
spraying each other with (ahem) hoses.
The crowd shrieks and covers their eyes
only to peep between their fingers.
It's like watching a car crash
without the cars: the bumps,
the grinds, the explosions.
Their faces painted in permanent
expressions of shock and delight,
they grimace and moan
almost like real
people

while the band plays furiously on.

Windows

Someone said windows are the soul of a house.
My house is dirty and full of spiders.

Windows are a stage
on which the drama of our lives
is played out.
The reviews are not good.

My neighbors are acting out
their lives in their front yard.
Screaming at the kids,
slamming doors,
and driving away
at unreasonable speeds.

The entire world
is their window.

A Greek chorus
of dogs proclaims
their every move.

How His Girlfriend Said Goodbye

Somewhere at the edge of the universe
where the first stars
are still dust

racing away from a loud noise

somewhere
just about there
a heart-shaped telephone
is ringing that no one will answer,
you bastard.

A Good Word

What is said
about a man
(or a woman)
precedes them
like the high school band
precedes fire trucks
in a Fourth of July parade.
Not everything has to be in tune
to be heard or to say something
the heart can feel.

Aftermath

Literally, the calculation
of damage done.
Tree through window.
Street sign, twisted
out of the ground
and hurled a hundred
and twenty feet
into a green Honda Civic.
Water, where water
was never meant to be.
The calculus of disaster.
The arithmetic
of every day.

Meat

I'm sorry. I didn't know
the cow/pig/bird/fish
we are eating. I only know
the meat was the right
shape & size for what
I was cooking,
not the anonymous
and probably reluctant
donor of our feast. Tonight
it's burgers. As far
from resembling a cow
as this bun is from a field
filled with strands of wheat.
Nothing shared but its color
and a faint trace of remorse
I have grown to ignore. But I am glad
I didn't know Mabel,
Bessie, or (god forbid) Frank.
Glad this meal comes unattached
to the violence it predicates. Glad
I am neither hunter nor gatherer
but ignorant beneficiary of both.

Interlude

Between one heartbeat and the next
is a silence, like a single book
propped on a bookshelf
to prove it is really
what it seems.
No one reads the book.
No one even knows its title.
Because no one ever
enters the room, afraid
they may overstay their welcome.

History

Every poem has been written before
at least fifteen times.
Every song
sung better.

The Neanderthals discovered caves
already painted with the story of their lives.
They invented fire
over and over again.

And you & I
whisper the same sweet nothings
we were born with.

Dust

Our personal historian.
The blanket we shrug off each morning.
The bones of extinct dinosaurs
covering our bones.
And Time, the charlady,
asleep in the corner.

Telling Stories

The trees are telling stories.
They are waving their arms
and snapping their fingers
to get our attention.

The birds are listening.
The squirrels run into the street.

My neighbor, walking his dog,
is not concerned. The three year-old
next door screams
and drives his Hot Wheels
into his father's leg over and over.
Predictable.

The trees burst into flame
in yellows and oranges. On the horizon
the clouds stack up like overdue bills.
Someone has to be wrong.

My Life as a Video Game

At first it's easy:
run, jump, and collect
health and ammunition.
But after the first couple of levels
things get ugly.
Large birds follow me everywhere
pecking at my innards.
My apartment is under attack
from cybernetic alien bug people
and my neighbor is a zombie.
This puny handgun is useless!
And the game keeps restarting
at the same location:
where the alarm sounds
and I reach for the light switch
which is armed to go off
in my face.

Self-Portrait at Fifty

More and more of my life is taken up by tasks
that do not enhance—but detract. From life, that is.

■ ■ ■

My friends are silent
because they are preoccupied
with their own pitiful stories.

■ ■ ■

The afterlife after this life
won't have much I missed.
A few game shows, a dinner party
with the unenviable . . .

■ ■ ■

I am aware of nothing
so much as the need to be.
This does not please me.
Being is overrated.

■ ■ ■

Metaphor is dead.
Similes annoy me.
I have been mistreated
by language.

■ ■ ■

(Puppets.)

■ ■ ■

The other side of wherever I am
is not very far away.

■ ■ ■

What does my life mean?
Another useless question
shouted out from the balcony.

■ ■ ■

I am getting old.
My hair grows where I don't want it
and doesn't grow where I want it to.
A metaphor for life?
Hardly. Life itself.
Metaphors excluded.

■ ■ ■

You can say I'm looking for excuses.
Then, fine, I'm looking for excuses.

■ ■ ■

Alternate title: *talked to death*

What We Know of the Story So Far

One among us knows
what the others can only guess.
In China, the lucky numbers
are the reverse of here.
Everyone wants to get married
on the 9th. Avoid the 4th at all costs.
Our happiness is limited
only by our ability
to escape sad thoughts.
The nuclear reactor
is only 37 miles away.
The outlet pipes raise the temperature
of the surrounding estuary
attracting birds. We only have
19 years of productive life
left, according to a committee report.
The plovers are slowly returning
now that we have banned people and dogs
from the beaches where they nest.
It may be years before we know for sure.

Solitude

"Solitude is like rain"
        —Rilke

Which would imply
rain is lonely
or makes us lonely.
Or perhaps he was referring
to the separateness
of each drop, the same way
we are separate, one from another.
Or some such bullshit.
The fact that I am even talking
to you proves or disproves
any theories we may have
about human existence.
I wish I could hold you in my arms
and squeeze until pain and pleasure
meet in the middle and call a truce.
Really. We are so far apart
I can barely hear you
breathing. But
that one decibel,
that single audible,
is enough
to prove
we are neither alone

nor completely
separate
from the animals
we have become.

Three Variations on Li Po

1.

Step into the river. Swim.
Fish laugh at you
but your enemies can't
follow in their heavy armor.

2.

Step into the river.
Your ankles become fish.
Your hands are birds
and your head a mountain
shrouded in clouds.

3.

River. Fish.
Trees. Birds.
Mountains. Clouds.

Old Enough to Know Better

But not
knowing

anything
good

he laid claim to one half
of everything they owned.

Bastard
she said. He said

Bitch. And the names
continued through the night.

I gave up
the best

years of my life
for you, she screamed.

You should have
he replied

known better.

Theoretical

So, what if
Confucius were alive today

doing the rap thing
and living in East L.A.

Would he be more Snoop Dogg
or more like L. L. Cool J?

I'm putting my money on the Dogg.

Artist: unknown

Inside the box
is a box
I call "the box".
It is not a real box.
It is a model of a box.
On the wall next to the box
is a white index card
written in fine print
describing the contents
of the box and who created it.
We stand admiring the box
from a respectful distance.
Some admire the index card.
The line to get in stretches all the way
around the block.
When our turn is up
we go outside into the sunlight
and the company of flowers and trees
feeling strangely better about ourselves.

My Rival

The spiders in my house avoid me.
They know we are rivals.
Solitary, hunting
the dry remains
of what did not fear us
enough. And our fears?
Light, sound, movement
inside the heart that betrays weakness.
I set a table for one
in a house full of guests.
I read *Losers Digest*
and laugh at the stories
more miserable than my own.
I eye my neighbors suspiciously
jealous of their nonchalance.
We are bitter rivals.
Each to his own
corner, glum. Glum
with pride
as we sit knitting
a doily for the wooden box
we imagine one day
we will call our very own.

Snake Bite

Implies snake bit
which can be figurative
or the literal
pair of red incisions
that do not swell
at first, as the poison
races toward the heart.
The same could be said
of the figurative snake bit,
which will not kill you
but leaves you stunned
and unable to use the heart
for anything but
recrimination.
Wishing you could
suck the literal venom
out or die
from it.

Prayer

Fuck me over, Lord.
Screw the poor

bastards who show no fear.
The loveless, the disbelieving,
the not so meek, etc.
Tell us where to get off
and, if necessary,
give us a shove

in the proper direction.
Face it. I gave you plenty of cause
to curse me and scourge
my progeny. And for doing that
I thank you. I thank you
for the brakes that did not fail
and the fuse that did.
Thank you for the arc, the bare wires,
and the rain that stopped them.
Thank you for the darkness
gone uninterrupted
and the light
I curse each morning.
Curse and savor.

Aphorisms

After Achille Chaveé

The city never sleeps. Its dreams won't allow it.

If you think you are alone, your shadow is looking the
other way.

While you sleep, your shadow is . . . wait! How do you know?

Darkness is another shadow, larger than your own.

If there are no angels, there are no devils.

The man who approaches you on the street and asks for a
dollar for a cup of coffee may be a saint. Or what a saint
looks like from a great distance.

After Li Bai

Lying drunk in a flower bed
I pour a glass for my friends,
the chrysanthemums. And the moon,
I would offer to buy the moon
a round for its round, sad face,
to little effect. It is late.
My pockets are full of dirt.
And my wife is screaming
from the porch
for me to come in
and stop embarrassing her
in front of the neighbors.
The Chinese poets
have nothing to offer
on this predicament.
Cowards, or wiser
men than me.
They know
to let the soul rejoice
inwardly, and to drink
quietly in the mountains
where the birds' complaints
sound like music.

Pencil

A tunnel
dark at both ends.
If you listen carefully
you can hear someone
calling. It is difficult
to make out what
they are saying
but you think
there has been
an accident. You think
there is something
you need
to write down.

Scissors

Skeleton of an extinct predator.
The last undiscovered dinosaur.
It reminds us that we too once had claws.
So comfortable in the hand,
it makes everything around you
look like it needs cutting.
A bird, raised in captivity,
that hasn't flown for years,
asleep, its mouth ajar
dreaming of clouds and sky.

Brick

1.

The thing, like the word
itself, is opaque. Indivisible.
Dumb as (in much the same way)
the word *stump*.

2.

Look closer.
If you had never seen it before,
if you didn't know the heft of it
or hadn't scraped your knuckles
against its side, time after time,

you might mistake it for a sponge
or a very old loaf of bread.

3.

The definition of inertia.
A face only gravity could love.
The first and last weapon.
What remains of civilization
when civilization inevitably fails.

Machu Picchu, Chichen Itza, Sarajevo.

Ghazal

The darkness isn't permanent.
But you cannot prove it.

Driving at night without the lights on.
You might as well be in outer space.

Your life is short.
It is always trying to catch up.

Haiku

Slow.

Deaf.

Child.

My Feelings

I do not talk
about my feelings
easily.

Four dead in stage collapse.

There are places in my house
I have never visited.
The shelf in the hall closet
behind where the iron and the bottle
of spray starch sit
and wait. The gap
next to the furnace
where dust gathers to heal.

Apartment house in flames,
toddler escapes.

These stories do not reassure me.
The heart collects dust.
I fear

what I have waited
so many years to say
is no longer true.

Fox

Fox where fox
doesn't belong.
Which is not to say
there is no place in the modern world
for quick brown fox and his brethren.
But my back yard is neither literary
nor linguistic. Besides,
many lazy dogs live
in this neighborhood.

But there he was easily mistaken
for a cat (of which there are also many)
except sleeker, red, and pointy
eared. The epitome of fox
in the quintessential
suburban landscape.
Only a swing set missing
to make the picture complete.

I saw him, but he
didn't see me, behind glass
fifteen or more feet
above eye level. To him
I was as abstract as an alphabet:
neither threat not food.
And the boundaries
we humans cherish

mean even less. So
he paused, listening
for something

more tangible than syllables.
Something small and alive
with fear

passing through.

There's No Title to This

He said
and began to recite
the nameless
words and ideas
which stand in
for the name of the thing
—because there are no ideas
but in things. And the namelessness
of the thing was the story
he told as he recited
word for word
what we began to suspect
was our story or that
of someone we knew
but could not name.

Outlook

Eye—hurts.
Back, not so much.
But the bruise on my arm
reminds me
I am not super
human. Or simply
human enough
to avoid
accidents. If only
I could stop
rubbing
my eye
long enough
I could see
(once the swelling
goes down) the truth
of the situation:
none of the parts
are happy

but as a whole
the outlook

is bright.

Notes

The title and certain facts from the poem "How to Clean an Oil-Slicked Penguin" are taken from an article of the same name that appeared in the BBC magazine.